WILD CATS

WILD CATS

Mike and Peggy Briggs

Bath · New York · Singapore · Hong Kong · Cologne · Delhi
Melbourne · Amsterdam · Johannesburg · Auckland · Shenzhen

This edition published by Parragon in 2011

Parragon
Queen Street House
4 Queen Street
Bath, BA1 1HE, UK

Produced by Atlantic Publishing

Photographs courtesy of
Photolibrary.com
(see page 255 for copyright details)
Text © Parragon Books Ltd 2006

ISBN 978-1-4454-3424-7

Printed in Indonesia

CONTENTS

INTRODUCTION 7

BIG CATS OF AFRICA AND EURASIA

LIONS 10

CHEETAHS 48

LEOPARDS 84

WILDCATS, LYNXES, AND OTHER SMALLER CATS 120

TIGERS 152

BIG CATS OF THE AMERICAS

LYNXES AND BOBCATS 178

MOUNTAIN LIONS AND FLORIDA PANTHERS 195

JAGUARS AND OTHER SOUTH AMERICAN CATS 219

BIBLIOGRAPHY 254

PICTURE ACKNOWLEDGMENTS 255

INTRODUCTION

Cats that swim underwater to catch their prey; cats as big as prehistoric saber-toothed tigers; cats that can pluck birds from the air and cats that can walk on desert sand hot enough to fry an egg – they are all out there in the wild, some in healthy numbers and some on the point of extinction.

Some wild cats have been revered since ancient times and some have been discovered only recently; but they all have a particular grace and sinuous, latent power that, even in the humble farmyard tabby, can spellbind an observer – and terrify a potential victim.

Wild cats come in a variety of sizes and colors but are all generally of the same shape (although some are almost weasel-like) and are instantly recognizable as alternative versions of our domestic cat. They are all members of the animal family called the Felidae which is itself broken down into sub-families, or genera, and then further into individual species within each genus (although these divisions are subject to much debate and taxonomists either lump species together or split them apart, according to personal preferences). It is agreed, however, that species are different when they cannot interbreed to produce fertile offspring: although lions and tigers can breed to create "ligers" and "tigons," these creatures are sterile, so lions and tigers are separate species.

So, while the cheetah is the only member of the Acinonyx genus and the clouded leopard the sole Neofelis, the Panthera group encompasses all the "big cats" (lion, tiger, jaguar, and leopard) and the Felis genus contains most of the other smaller cats, with a handful of other genera covering the remainder. There are other differences apart from breeding incompatibility: big cats can roar (having a softer hyoid bone in their throats) but can purr only on the outbreath; small cats have partially hairless nose pads; they feed lying down beside large prey, rather than crouching; and their pupils are slit-shaped rather than round.

Apart from elegance and beauty, all cats share a consummate ability to hunt: they are the ultimate carnivore, with highly efficient eyes and ears, sensitive whiskers, silent feet, perfectly camouflaged coats, sharp teeth and claws, and wonderful coordination, agility, and balance. Yet, despite such advantages, they have to work very hard for their food and often spend a tiring night on the prowl, sometimes making several fruitless attacks, for no reward.

The fact remains, though, that wild cats, even the smallest ones, are impressive, rather frightening killers with an unnerving independence and a disdain for humans not found in other wild animals. This special aura has made them obvious choices as earthly representations of powerful gods and the subjects of much superstition, mythology, and folklore. The cult of the jaguar god, for instance, was central to the Mayan civilization in South America and persisted long after the Mayans had gone into decline. Lions and leopards feature regularly in European heraldic coats of arms and the tiger is synonymous with the vibrant, thrusting economies of the Far East. The fat of tigers and lions is still thought to cure many ills (including earache and rheumatism) and the lion was (and possibly still is) the source of a particularly lucky charm for the Swahili people of southern Africa.

Unfortunately, the lion and its cousins have no such protection against attack by man. Wild cats are under threat both directly – being killed for their fur, for trophies and for body parts – and indirectly as their habitats are being eaten away by agriculture and industry and their prey is wiped out or driven off. None of the big cats has an entirely safe foothold in an increasingly rapacious world and conservationists are having to fight an often very ugly war to save them from extinction.

The future of all the wild cats will be made more secure by greater appreciation, knowledge, and understanding, and it is hoped that this book will help contribute to this and allow more people to fall under the spell of these wonderful creatures.

Note: unless otherwise stated, lengths given are head-and-body lengths, excluding tail.

BIG CATS OF
AFRICA
AND
EURASIA

LIONS

The symbol of power, steadfastness, aggression, and valor, the lion (*Panthera leo*) has a long association with the political, artistic, and mythical dealings of mankind.

Once far more widespread, it has been extinct in Europe for 2,000 years. Ten subspecies now live in Africa and one – the critically endangered Asiatic lion (*Panthera leo persica*) – in the small Gir Forest preserve of India. Most African lions live in protected areas in the east and south, with a declining number in the west. The African lion population fell by almost 90 percent in the 20 years to 2003, from 200,000 to just over 20,000, and some experts think it might be on the brink of extinction.

The greatest threats are sport hunting and conflicts with livestock farmers. There have also been demands for culls as the number of attacks on humans has risen in areas where traditional prey is on the decline and agricultural pressure is increasing. In Tanzania, for example, 563 people were killed and at least 308 injured by lions between 1990 and 2005 – a significant increase on comparable periods – and 20 Ethiopians were killed in just one month in 2005.

Adult males weigh an average of about 420 lb (190 kg), with the heaviest on record (in Kenya) weighing almost 600 lb (272 kg). Females average 277 lb (126 kg). Males are about 4 feet (1.2 m) high at the shoulder and females 3 feet 8 inches (1.1 m). Body length ranges from $7\frac{1}{2}$ to $10\frac{1}{2}$ feet (2.4–3.3 m) and tail length from 24 to 39 inches (60–100 cm).

Left: A lioness perches in the branches of a tree. The African lion is usually associated with plains or savannah habitats, but it is capable of surviving in a variety of other environments, including along the fringes of desert areas and in forested and mountainous regions. A small population of lions lives in the Bale mountains in Ethiopia at an altitude of some 13,000 feet (4,000 m). The lion does not, however, thrive in true desert conditions nor in the rainforest.

Previous pages: Male lions are the only cats with manes and these two are only just beginning to develop theirs. Lions are also unique in having a tuft at the end of their tails but otherwise their tawny-yellow coats are probably the plainest of all cats.

Opposite: Lions drink regularly if there is water available, but they can get all their moisture just from their food, including plants. In the Kalahari desert, for example, lions will eat the tsama melon – a juicy treat found just beneath the surface.

Above: Each of the females in this group, ranged round a water hole, will have been born in the same ancestral home ground and will stay there to breed. Lions are the only cats to live in extended family groups – or prides – like this and the reasons are unclear. It might be because they can pool their hunting skills, more easily defend their young, keep out intruders, or insure they get at least some food, even if shared.

Opposite: A lioness moves her cub to a new hiding place, carrying it by the scruff of the neck. One of the biggest threats to lion cubs are marauding males seeking a pride to take over. A new dominant male will kill all the suckling cubs of a pride to insure the survival of his genes. Any lioness that loses her cubs like this (many fight to the death to prevent it happening) will become fertile again after a couple of weeks and mate with the new pride leader.

Above: Youngsters rough each other up as they play-fight in preparation for hunting, but because lions are so powerful and capable of killing or critically injuring each other, pride members seldom fight in earnest.

Previous pages: A mother tends her young cub which seems rather bemused by life. Cubs are born (after a gestation period of about 14 weeks) with spots which usually fade as they get older.

Previous pages: The youngsters have a better chance of survival when related females in the same pride reproduce at the same time and cross-suckle. This synchronization of breeding is common and cubs are often raised in crèches like this one where the whole pride helps to raise several litters at once.

Above and opposite: Cubs are kept in hiding by their mother until they are about eight weeks old. Although they can walk 15 days after birth and run after just one month they are still vulnerable to predators. Cubs weigh 2–4 lb (1–2 kg) at birth and their eyes open after about 11 days. Though weaned at 7–10 months they are still dependent on adults until they are at least 16 months old.

Left: Females live about 15–16 years, some 5–6 years longer than males. In captivity, lions live about 13 years and the oldest on record was 30.

Previous pages: The phrase "rubbing along together" could have been invented for lions: they do an awful lot of it. This female is rubbing herself against a (rather long-suffering) young male's head to deposit scent. Sexes rub each other in greeting, sometimes quite forcefully. They also have scent glands in the corners of their mouths and rub heads as a mark of bonding. Less pleasantly, males spray each other with urine as a mark of friendship.

Opposite: Lions copulate about 3,000 times for each cub that survives more than a year. During the four-day period when she is ready to breed a female mates more than twice an hour with whichever males win her consent. Consent is hard won, with much snarling and cuffing from both sides. During mating the successful male grasps the female's neck with his teeth but the female crouches passively once she has succumbed to his advances.

Above: Where there is bountiful prey lions spend approximately 20 hours per day sleeping and become active in the late afternoon and at night, when their roar is most likely to be heard. Only lions, tigers, leopards, and jaguars roar – and lions roar the most, sometimes in choruses involving the whole pride. Roaring is a vital part of a male lion's territorial demarcation and can be heard up to 5 miles (8 km) away.

Right: A lion's tongue is covered with rough spines which act like a comb during grooming and also scrape meat off bones. An after-meal clean-up will also sometimes involve using the dew claw on a front leg as a toothpick.

Previous pages: Females apparently prefer to mate with males that have darker manes, and science backs them up: a survey of adult males showed dark manes were linked to better nutrition, good health, higher testosterone levels, and longevity.

Females have no choice of mate when their pride is taken over by new males. Young males are expelled from their prides at about $2\frac{1}{2}$ years old and after 2–3 years of nomadic life join forces with one or a few other males (usually brothers) to fight for ownership of a pride. They in their turn will be ousted after about $2\frac{1}{2}$ years.

Left: A female on the prowl through a marsh. Females do almost all the hunting, sometimes alone but usually in groups when their roles — either driving the quarry or spearheading the attack — will often change according to prey type. Individual lionesses appear to lead the hunt for warthogs, for example, but usually remain passive when buffalo are the target.

Opposite: A lion's teeth are well adapted for killing and eating its prey. The canine teeth have evolved in size and spacing to slip between the neck vertebrae of their preferred prey and sever the spinal cord. The back teeth work like scissors to cut up the meat (rather than grinding) and the lion swallows its food without chewing.

Above: Two females bring down a buffalo – one seizing its throat and one its hindquarters – in an operation that might take several minutes. Groups of lions kill more prey overall (with a success rate of 30 percent per hunt) whereas individuals succeed only 17 percent of the time – but the individuals end up with more meat each.

Right: Zebra is a regular large prey species along with buffalo, wildebeest, roan antelope, sable, springbok, gemsbok, kob, impala, warthog, waterbuck, and hartebeest. Lions which cannot capture large prey will eat birds, fish, rodents, reptiles, amphibians, and even ostrich eggs. One pride living near Namibia's Skeleton Coast desert learned to prey and scavenge on Cape fur seals before being wiped out in 1991 by cattle herdsmen.

Following pages: This juvenile, joining the feast on a roan antelope, will be on the lookout for intruders – particularly spotted hyenas (*Crocuta crocuta*), which are the only predator that will attack and even kill adult lions.

Left and above: According to radio-telemetry studies carried out in 1993, there are just over 200 Asiatic lions left. Hunting helped wipe them out: the diary of an English officer recorded that he shot 300 lions in 1857 alone. By 1900 the Asiatic lion was confined to the Gir where it was protected by the Nawab of Junagadh.

It is slightly smaller than the African lion with a shorter mane, thicker elbow and tail tufts, and a longitudinal skin fold on its stomach. An adult male (*left*) will grow to 350–420 lb (160–190 kg), and a female (*above*) to 220–265 lb (100–120 kg). The record total length, including tail, is 9½ feet (2.92 m). Asiatic lionesses live an average of 17–18 years, and males 16 years.

Following pages: The Imperial lion depicted on British coins (and on the British Royal Coat of Arms, "fighting the unicorn for the crown") and the lion to which Christians were thrown in Rome's Colosseum are the same beast, and now extinct. The Barbary lion (*Panthera leo leo*), the largest lion subspecies weighing 500 lb (225 kg) or more, lived in the Atlas Mountain forests of North Africa. The last wild Barbary lion was killed in Morocco in the early 1920s and a few specimens retaining its features remain in zoos.

CHEETAHS

The cheetah (*Acinonyx jubatus*) — the fastest four-legged creature — owes its speed to its remarkably flexible spine which allows it to bound far farther and with greater acceleration than other cats. Its stamina in a chase is limited, however, by its ability to dissipate body heat. In theory a pursuit of 550 yards (500 m) will generate a lethal temperature level and few chases of more than 450 yards (400 m) have been witnessed.

Cheetahs are mostly found in the open and semi-open grasslands of eastern and southwestern Africa, although they once lived in many parts of Africa and Asia. A few have been spotted in Iran but they have disappeared altogether from India. There were once about 100,000 in the wild but numbers are now down to as few as 9,000–15,000. It has always been popular as a pet, however, and many are kept in zoos and wildlife parks.

Like most cat species, the cheetah can display varied colors and markings. The king cheetah is one such mutant but there have been other examples, including a white cheetah with blue spots which was once owned by the Moghul emperor Jahangir.

This graceful hunter has unusually good vision, even for a cat, and many wildlife tourists have enjoyed the sight of a cheetah in a typical posture: perched on a rock or knoll, peering out over the savannah in search of its next meal.

Above: Like most cats, cheetah cubs are born blind and some time within the next week or so these five-day-old cubs will be opening their eyes to study the world around them. Weighing only 8½ oz (250–300 g) at birth, they have some growing to do before they can venture from their den.

Opposite: Cheetah litters can number as many as eight cubs although the average is three to five. This two-month-old cub might be the last from its litter as the cubs have an 80–90 percent mortality rate. This might seem harsh but it is nature's way of balancing the species so enough deer survive to feed the next generation.

Previous pages: These three-week-old cheetah cubs have probably just got their first teeth but it will be another few weeks before they start to eat meat and six months before they are fully weaned.

Left: Keeping a watchful eye as they drink, this family group will stay together until the cubs are 13–20 months old.

Previous pages: Young cheetahs have a long, woolly mantle or mane covering their backs, helping to camouflage them in the open savannah. Still clearly visible on these six-week-old cubs, the mane will have practically disappeared and their dorsal spots developed by the time they are four months old.

Above: Many cheetah cubs are taken by lions or leopards, so the mother moves them every five days or so. Leaving them alone while she hunts for food, she will cautiously wait until dark before returning to her young in their den.

Opposite: The cheetah's characteristic tear-stained face is accounted for by a moving Zulu story about a lazy hunter who stole a litter of cubs to train to make his life easier. The heartbroken mother sobbed piteously for a day and a night until heard by a tribesman. She told him her story; he related it to the elders, and the hunter was driven from the village for the dishonor of hunting with anything other than personal strength and skill. The cubs were returned to their mother but her tears had stained her face for life — and for generations to come.

Previous pages: Many cats use their tail as an aid to balance, but the cheetah, with a longer-than-average tail of 24–35 inches (60–90 cm), also uses it as a rudder as it swerves in pursuit of its quarry.

Above: With long legs, a flexible spine and a lithe body, the cheetah takes a mere two seconds to accelerate from 0–45 mph (0–70 kph). It can sprint at speeds of up to 60 mph (95 kph) but cannot keep this up for any length of time. Most chases only last about 20 seconds and the cheetah is usually so exhausted that it needs half an hour before recovering sufficiently to be able to eat or drag the carcass back to its cubs.

Opposite: The cheetah cannot retract its claws – an advantage during a high-speed chase, as the claws provide traction like a runner's spikes, but a disadvantage in that they are permanently blunt.

Above: When first officially verified (after numerous rumors) in the 1920s, the king cheetah was heralded as a separate species, *Acinonyx Rex*. The striking markings, where spots have merged into broken stripes, make the king cheetah easy to identify even though only a few have been seen in the wild. It is now known that this is merely a rare pattern mutation, similar to that producing a black leopard.

Opposite: The king cheetah has been recorded as found in only a few restricted areas, mainly around Zimbabwe, although one skin was reported to have been brought from west Africa. This cat has been successfully bred in captivity and some cases have been recorded of both normal and king cheetah markings appearing in the same litter.

Following pages: The cheetah is the same length as the other African spotted cat, the leopard (43–59 inches (110–150 cm) excluding tail), but there the similarity ends. With its long, slender legs, the cheetah stands about 10 inches (25 cm) taller than a leopard and at 84–138 lb (38–63 kg) weighs far less.

Above: According to a bushman legend, the wild dog gave the cheetah its paws as a token of esteem after seeing the cheetah's compassion when its rival broke a leg during a race to decide the fastest animal. The cheetah's paws are certainly different from those of other cats: the pads are harder and have ridges like the tread of a tire – providing plenty of purchase for fast cornering.

Opposite: A good stretch is essential to maintain a healthy, flexible spine. The cheetah needs to keep its spine in tiptop condition to be able to swerve after its prey at high speeds.

Above: Rather than pounce on the back of its prey, this cheetah is using its prominent dew claws to spike or trip up the unfortunate impala. It takes years of practice to become a proficient hunter and young cheetahs often fail to crouch low enough to remain hidden.

Opposite: Lacking the jaw strength to break the neck of this Thompson's gazelle in the way a lion would, the cheetah has suffocated its victim by enclosing the nose and mouth or grasping the throat. This method is so efficient that the prey is often unmarked and the skin unbroken.

Previous pages: The cheetah's spots are solid, rather than forming rosettes like those of a leopard. This cat got its name from the Sanskrit word *chita* meaning "spotted one."

Previous pages: The cheetah isn't strong enough to heave its dinner into the safety of a tree, as a leopard does, so has to drag it to the nearest cover and hope to have time to eat its fill before scavengers move in. To avoid other large predators, the cheetah often hunts during the hottest part of the day when lions and hyenas are enjoying a siesta.

Opposite: It might be admired for its speed, grace, and beauty but the cheetah's table manners leave much to be desired. This cheetah cub is no exception, pausing with the remains of its dinner splattered over its face.

Above: Nuzzling is not just a gesture of affection but frequently a mutual grooming operation to clean up after finishing a meal.

Right: About to dine, this cheetah will hope to have its fill before vultures alert lions and hyenas to the fact that fresh impala is on the menu. Cheetahs are the lightweights of the big cats and are not sufficiently aggressive to defend their kill, losing about 12 percent to lions. They do not scavenge the remains of other predators' kills but hunt afresh every few days.

Following pages: Cheetah cubs leave home before they are two years old and litter-mates often stay together for six months or so before venturing off on their own. Any females in this group in Etosha National Park, Namibia, will go off to seek their fortune when they reach sexual maturity, leaving the males to form their own brotherhood band.

A lone cheetah has a 70 percent success rate when hunting, second only to a wild dog, but this rate is increased when males hunt in groups.

Left: Throughout history, cheetahs have been tamed and kept as pets, status symbols, or trained hunters. In the Middle Ages European nobility indulged in this exotic sport, taking the cheetahs on horseback to the hunting field, sitting on a cushion behind their handlers. Adults were easier to train than cubs and elaborate traps were set to capture them. Akbar the Great of India was reputed to have kept 9,000 hunting cheetahs during his reign, training many of them himself.

LEOPARDS

The leopard (*Panthera pardus*) is the most adaptable of the wild cats, ranging throughout sub-Saharan Africa, the Middle East, India, the Far East, the Himalayas, and China to the very northeast of Russia. It can live anywhere with an annual rainfall of 2 inches (50 mm) or more or with a regular water supply.

Despite being hunted for trophies, furs, and "medicinal" body parts, being persecuted by farmers and deprived of its habitat, it has survived where other big cats have disappeared. It is nevertheless under threat in many regions: eight of the 20 sub-species are listed as endangered or critically endangered by the World Conservation Union (IUCN), with some – like the Arabian (*P.p. nimr*), Amur (*P.p. orientalis*), and Anatolian (*P.p. tulliana*) – nearing extinction. The sub-Saharan population is stable at an estimated 714,000 but poachers are reducing numbers dramatically in Asia.

Males are up to 50 percent larger than females, ranging from a total length of $9\frac{1}{2}$ feet (2.92 m) and weight of 200 lb (91 kg) – recorded in Rwanda and South Africa respectively – down to just 6 feet (1.8 m) and 60 lb (28 kg) for a pygmy leopard (*Felis pardus nanopardus*) found in Somalia.

The clouded leopard (*Neofelis nebulosa*) lives in the primary evergreen tropical rainforests of Asia. Although illegally hunted it is actually most under threat from deforestation. Sized between the big and small cats, adults weigh 24–44 lb (11–20 kg).

The endangered snow leopard (*Uncia uncia*) is found only in the mountains of central Asia and the Himalayas but is losing its habitat to livestock grazing. There are between 4,500 and 7,300 left in the wild. Males grow to a maximum length of $7\frac{1}{2}$ feet (2.3 m) and weight of 120 lb (55 kg).

Right: The leopard has extremely good eyesight, particularly in low light when it can see six times better than a human. This, coupled with hearing twice as acute as humans', allows it to pinpoint prey at its favorite hunting period between dusk and dawn.

Following pages: The leopard often hauls its catch, like this gazelle, up into a tree to avoid it being stolen by other competing carnivores (tree-stored meat also lasts about four times longer than kills kept on the ground). This requires enormous strength, particularly in the neck muscles: leopards have been seen dragging young giraffe of up to 275 lb (125 kg) – 2–3 times heavier than the leopard – more than 16 feet (5 m) up.

Opposite: The smallest of the four "Big Cats," the leopard is itself at risk from other creatures such as hyena and even bands of chimpanzees. It seeks safety in the trees where it can sleep in peace.

Right: Among the most agile of climbers, leopards, unlike domestic cats, can also descend a tree head first, gripping with their long, retractable claws.

Following pages: This is just a tiny leap for a leopard. It is second only to the mountain lion in its jumping ability and a leopard was once seen to launch itself more than 23 feet (7 m) down into a road cutting and bound instantly some 10 feet (3 m) up the other side.

Left: In Africa and India leopards mate all year, with peaks around the birth season of their principal prey, but in China and Siberia they mate only in January and February. The gestation period is 90–105 days.

Opposite: Litters can number up to six but are more usually two or three cubs, and the first-year survival rate is just 40–50 percent, so most mothers have just one cub to care for.

94

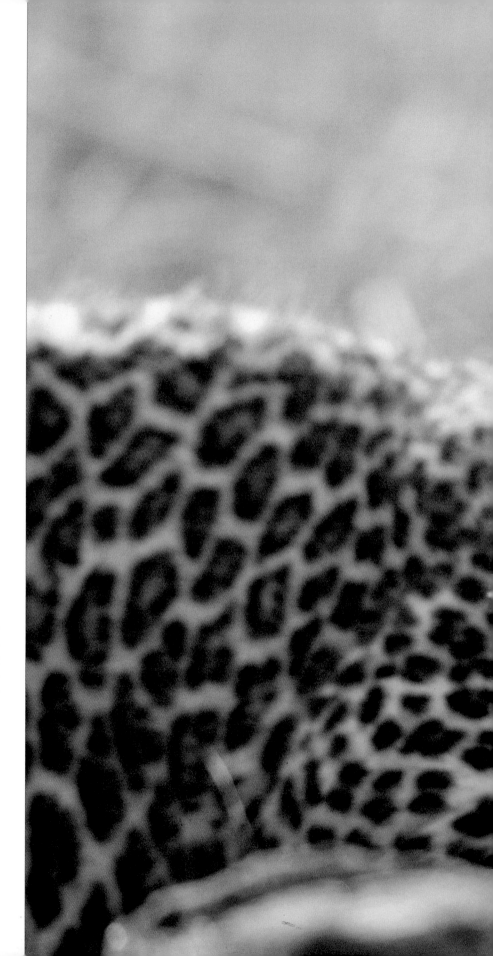

Right: This cuddly-looking cub will soon learn to kill. Youngsters start killing small prey at about five months and can fend for themselves at one year but usually stay with their mother for up to two years.

Previous pages: Holding them by the scruff of the neck or the loose skin on their back, the female leopard regularly moves her young from one hiding place to another every few days to protect them from lions, hyenas, and even male leopards.

Opposite: Despite tales of man-eating tigers it is actually the leopard which is more inclined to kill humans. Its varied diet and adaptability mean it is more likely to live near human habitation and to wander into villages and take whatever it can, including dogs, domestic livestock — and villagers. The man-eating leopard of Rudraprayag in India killed at least 125 people over nine years until it was shot in 1926.

Above: The leopard uses its powerful jaws to crush the throat and suffocate its victims rather than making an attack to the back of the neck.

Left: A mother patiently allows her juvenile offspring to use her as a climbing frame while they hone their hunting skills. Leopards are consummate stalkers, often coming to within touching distance of their prey before they make their final leap. Their patience and stealth are legendary and they seldom have to engage in tiring chases as they manage to maneuver to such close quarters.

Above: Black — or melanistic — leopards, also known confusingly as black panthers, are often found in the same litter as normally marked ones. Most inhabit the moist, dense forest of Burma, southwest China, Assam, Nepal, and some parts of southern India. They are scarce, though not unknown, in tropical Africa, and found mainly in the forests of Mount Kenya and the Aberdares.

Opposite: Contrary to popular belief, black leopards are no more ferocious than those with spots — they simply look more menacing.

Right: Although melanistic leopards appear completely black, their spots can still be seen, in certain reflecting light, as dark black rosettes on a lighter, dark brown background.

Leopard coloration generally is highly varied: from the creams and grays of the desert leopards, through the rusty reds and yellows of those on the savannah and the dark golds of the rainforest species to the deep browns of those in the mountains. Spot patterns are equally diverse.

Following pages: Whether melanistic or more conventionally spotted, having such a beautiful coat makes the leopard a prime target for the guns of poachers. Man is this cat's biggest enemy and some 50,000 leopards were killed in East Africa alone to satisfy the fur trade in the early 1960s.

Opposite: The clouded leopard, which is protected throughout much of its range, could just as easily be called the snake leopard as its markings and head shape give it a definite reptilian look.

Above: Its markings hide the clouded leopard in its jungle home where it preys on birds, primates, and small mammals, as well as larger creatures, such as porcupines, deer, and wild boar.

Left: The clouded leopard looks more like a small version of a Big Cat than other small felidae. It is set apart from all the other cats (and therefore given its own genus) by its teeth: it has the largest canine teeth (in relation to its size), with a gap behind them that allows it to take large bites out of its victims. The canines are also very sharp along their back edges – just like those of the saber-toothed tigers of prehistory.

Following pages: Although it will tolerate water, the clouded leopard is more at home in the trees where its agility rivals that of the South American margay. It can race headlong down tree trunks and even hang upside down from horizontal branches by its hind feet.

113

Above: Snow leopard cubs are born in late spring or early summer and their first few weeks are sometimes spent hidden in rock crevices.

Opposite: The snow leopard incurs the wrath of the sparse population in its remote habitat by killing domestic livestock such as yak, sheep, goats, and horses. Nepalese herders were traditionally forbidden to roast meat in case the mountain god sent its "dog" (the leopard) to kill their animals. However, they were also forbidden to kill the leopard as all its "sins" (for killing stock) would be transferred to them. Nowadays herdsmen have no such qualms.

Following pages: Its short forelimbs and long hind legs allow the snow leopard to leap with great agility over the rocky terrain while its exceptionally long tail aids balance. It also wraps its body and face with its tail to keep warm and its large paws support it in deep snow.

WILD CATS LYNXES

—————— AND OTHER ——————

SMALLER CATS

Although big cats are more glamorous and tend to hog the limelight, the smaller wild cats are no less interesting and often live in closer harmony with mankind. Indeed, it is from one of them – the African wild cat – that our domestic cats are believed to be descended.

Smaller cats are found throughout Europe, Africa, and Asia, from the European wild cat (*Felis silvestris silvestris*) living in woods and forests everywhere except in Scandinavia to the most isolated cat of all, the Iriomote cat (*Prionailurus bengalensis*), found only on the small mountainous island of Iriomote, east of Taiwan. This cat was not discovered until 1967.

The area from Egypt to the Far East is particularly richly blessed, with the widespread jungle cat (*F. chaus*), the rusty-spotted cat (*P. rubiginosus*), and the fishing cat (*P. viverrinus*) as well as those not pictured here, including the hardy Indian desert cat (*F. s. ornata*), Pallas' cat (*Otocolobus manul*) with its massive body and short, stout legs, the vicious Bornean bay cat (*Catopuma badia*), the Chinese mountain cat (*F. bieti*) found right up to nearly 10,000 feet (3,000 m) and the strange flat-headed cat (*P. planiceps*) which looks more like a mink or otter.

In the deserts of the Middle East we find the sand cat (*F. margarita*), and Africa is home to three species: the serval (*Leptailurus serval*) in the plains and forests, the black-footed cat (*F. nigripes*) of the brushlands and semi-deserts of the south, and the African wild cat (*F.s. lybica*) which is found almost everywhere except the western rainforests.

Left: Apart from when defending its kill, the serval isn't particularly aggressive but males sometimes engage in an interesting ritual combat. Two sit facing each other, one putting its paws on its rival's chest. The opponent will bite at the paws to get them off but often one cat will back off rather than engage in a full-scale fight.

Above: This serval is spray-marking its territory, which could be anywhere from $3\frac{1}{2}$–12 sq miles (9–31 sq km). Male territories overlap those of two or three females and rivals are warned off by the scent of the urine. Typical habitats include reed beds or scrub with some cover, and the graceful serval is never found very far from water. The serval eats small mammals and one male was recorded devouring 28 frogs in three hours.

Following pages: The serval's long legs allow it to see over high grass but the huge ears, with distinctive "eye spots" on the back, are more useful in locating prey. Swiveling them around to catch sound, the serval can detect a mouse 20 feet (6 m) away. About the size of an Alsatian dog – 26–39 inches (67–100 cm) long – it is much lighter at 20–40 lb (9–18 kg).

Opposite: They look docile but these black-footed cats have a fierce reputation. Botswana folklore holds that this cat can fell a giraffe. More realistically, a black-footed cat has been documented catching a Cape hare weighing more than 3 lb (1.5 kg) – the same as the cat. One of the world's smallest wild cats and named for its paw markings, this nocturnal species weighs 2–4 lb (1–1.9 kg) and is 13–19½ inches (33–50 cm) long.

Above: The African wild cat is the ancestor of our domestic housecats and can be difficult to differentiate from a feral tabby. Markings and coat colors vary but the reddish-brown tint at the back of the ears is a distinguishing feature. Resting during the heat of the day, the solitary wild cat hunts rodents, insects, and birds at night to maintain its 9–11 lb (4–5 kg) bodyweight.

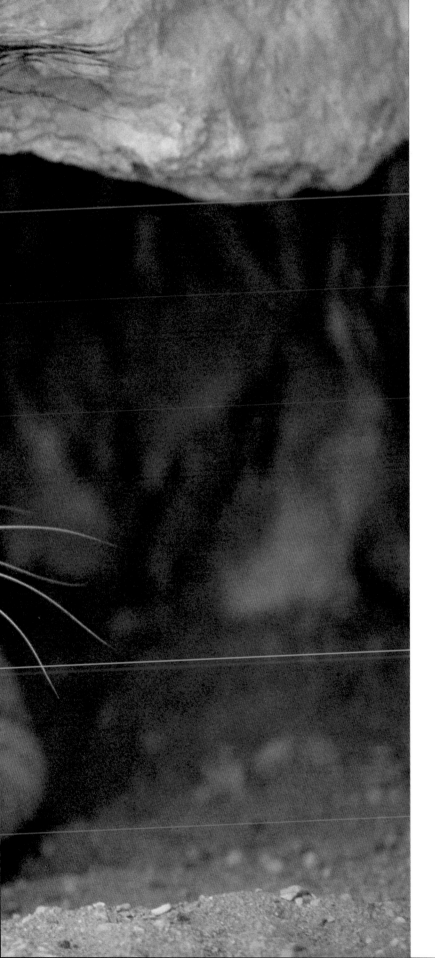

Left: Renowned as a fearless, powerful hunter, the caracal was once trained to hunt by Asian nobility. Perhaps the original "cat among the pigeons," this fast, agile, and athletic hunter can leap several feet into the air to catch birds, often knocking three or four from the air with its front paws before the flock flies high enough to escape.

Opposite: When suitors visit her territory, the female caracal makes her choice but is easily seduced and will take several partners, simply making the smaller or younger males wait their turn. After about 11 weeks, 2–3 cubs are born in a secluded den, sometimes underground if an obliging porcupine has moved house.

Right: The Turkish word "karakal," meaning "black ear," gave the handsome caracal its common name, and the tufts on those same, long ears prompted its other name of desert lynx. Weighing an average of 28 lb (13 kg), and 15½–19½ inches (40–50 cm) high, it is smaller than a lynx and doesn't actually inhabit the desert but does prefer the dry savannahs and acacia scrubland.

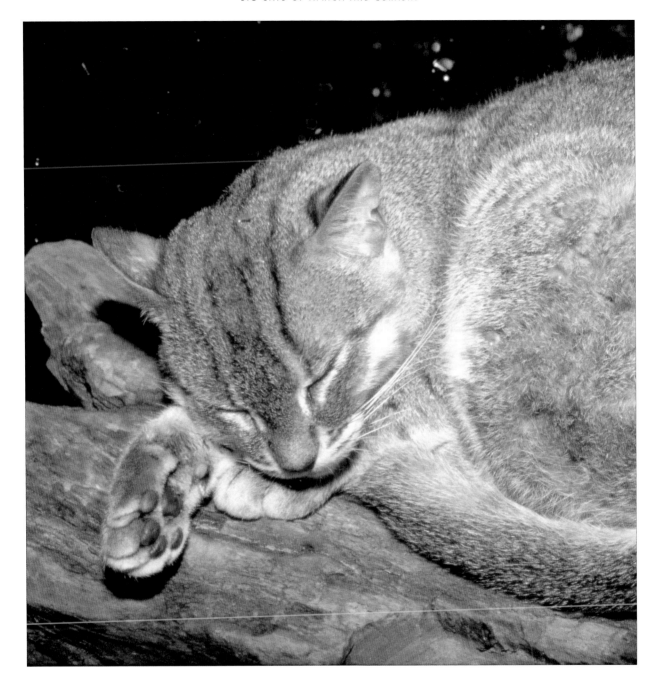

Opposite: A quick blow to the head is usually enough to stun a snake before the sand cat kills it by biting through its neck. Named for its perfectly camouflaged coat, this nocturnal desert cat is well adapted to its habitat. Although small – 3–7½ lb (1.5–3.4 kg) – it has large ears which help keep it cool, and dense hair on the soles of its feet to insulate against searing sand temperatures approaching 212°F (100°C).

Above: The rare, rusty-spotted cat, weighing 2½–3½ lb (1.1–1.6 kg), vies with the black-footed for the title of smallest wild cat. This elusive species has not been studied in detail although locals in India and Sri Lanka say the cats emerge after heavy rain to feed on frogs and rodents.

Opposite and above: With its long legs, long tail, and thick coat, Temminick's golden cat, sometimes called the Asian golden, is an impressive creature. It prefers humid habitats and its thrives in the forests of the eastern Himalayas, southern China and on the island of Sumatra.

Following pages: Mangrove swamps, reed beds, and tidal creeks – anywhere close to water – are typical habitats for the stocky fishing cat. Just 10–13 inches (25–33 cm) high at the shoulders, this powerful cat can weigh up to 26 lb (11.7 kg) and has a fearsome reputation. One large captive male killed a leopard after escaping from its cage and in Singapore a fishing cat was shot as it carried off a four-month-old baby.

Opposite: The aptly-named fishing cat has webbing between its toes and partly protruding claws which help it to catch fish. It will even dive in pursuit of prey, sometimes swimming underwater to snatch unsuspecting waterfowl from below by their legs.

Above: It is not surprising that the Chinese call the rare and beautiful marbled cat "the small clouded leopard," as its soft coat has similar exquisite markings. Weighing 4½–13 lb (2–6 kg), this nocturnal cat is only a third of the size of a clouded leopard but shares its long upper canines and is believed to be closely related.

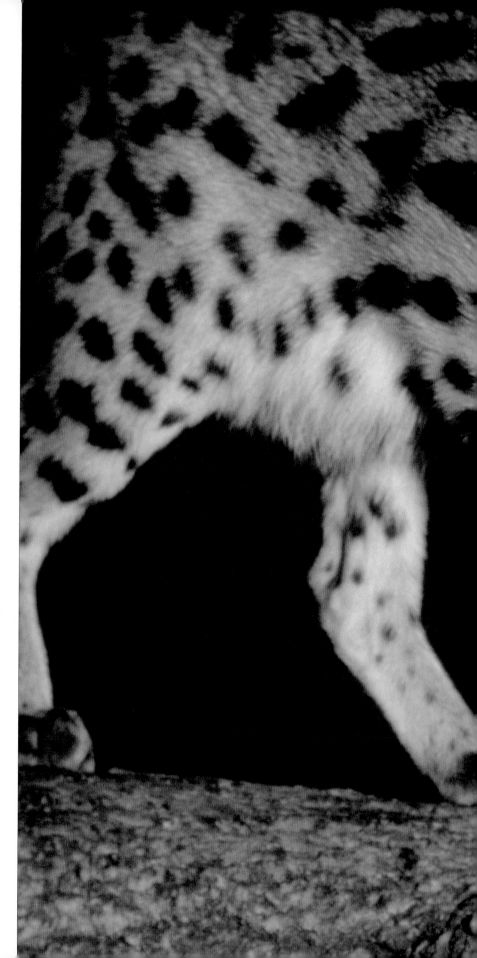

Previous pages: One of the most widely-distributed small wild cats, the jungle cat occurs in a variety of habitats. It can weigh up to 35 lb (16 kg) in Central Asia but in India it seldom exceeds 20 lb (9 kg). This daytime hunter searches fields and marshes for small mammals and birds, resorting to frogs or snakes if necessary. A competent swimmer, it was trained by ancient Egyptians to hunt water birds.

Right: A common species in southern Asia, the leopard cat is known as "chin-ch'ien mao" (the money cat) in China because its spots looked like coins. Like its namesake, this fierce little cat varies in size 24–35 inches (61–90 cm) and color (from dull gray to bright reddish) according to location.

Left: The sturdy European wild cat weighs 6½–17½ lb (3–8 kg), its thick winter coat making it appear larger than its African cousin. Frequenting woodland, mountains, and moors, it will prey on whatever species are readily available, from young wild boars, rabbits, and rodents to fish, birds, and even insects.

Above: Grooming keeps the wild cat's coat in good condition, making it warm in winter – a fact known to noblemen in the Middle Ages who used its skins to line their cloaks. Other parts of the wild cat were used for medicines, including an unbelievable potion of bear grease, onion juice, and powdered wild cat excrement, said to cure baldness.

Right: The wild cat has a reputation for aggressiveness, particularly when defending young, and has been known to see off foxes venturing too near its den. And the late photographer Geoffrey Kinns related an eyewitness account given to him of a wild cat jumping onto the back of an eagle which had snatched one of its kittens.

Left: In May or June the Eurasian lynx gives birth to 2–3 cubs weighing 10½ oz (300 g). The mother stays close to her den while the cubs are young as they don't walk for 3–4 weeks and it is five months before they are weaned.

Right: The Eurasian lynx prefers to prey on large members of the deer family and causes severe problems for the Scandinavian semi-domestic reindeer herds. Compensation for lynx kills is available in Finland but in Sweden, where annual losses can number 20,000–40,000, the local reindeer management association only receives payment for each lynx family on its grazing area. In Scandinavian folklore this secretive cat from the dark, coniferous forests drew the chariot of Freya, goddess of love and beauty.

Following pages: The Eurasian lynx is about twice the size of the Canadian lynx and the rare Iberian lynx (*Lynx pardinus*) of Spain and Portugal. With the characteristic short tail and long ear tufts of its cousins, the Eurasian lynx weighs in at 47½ lb (21.6 kg) for a male, and about 6½ lb (3 kg) lighter for a female.

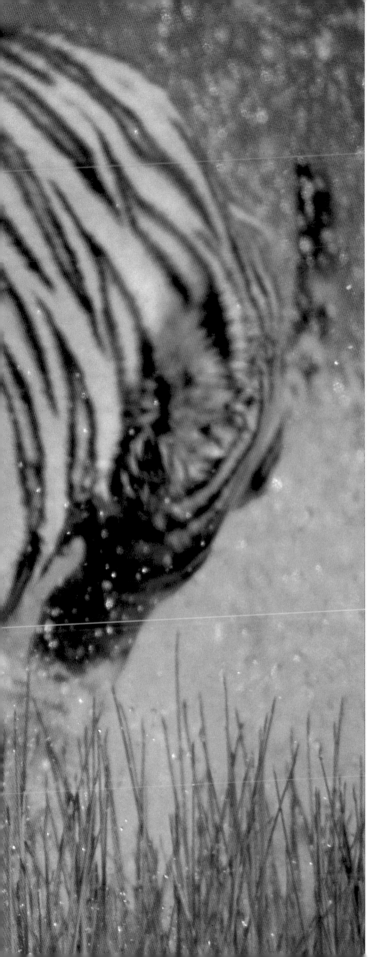

TIGERS

The tiger, the largest of the cats, was first brought to Europe in 19 B.C. and used in the games by the Romans or kept as a pet. After the Roman Empire fell it didn't reappear in Europe until 1478 but had already gained an undeserved reputation as a savage, cunning, yet cowardly beast, without the lion's pluck or bravery.

Persecuted by farmers and hunted throughout its range, its numbers soon declined: in 1930 there were 100,000 throughout Asia; in 1940 just 40,000; by 1970 just over 5,000; and a mere two years later an estimated 2,000. International conservation programs, anti-poaching measures, and the setting up of protected areas helped numbers recover to 6,400 by 1979. The population has fluctuated since then, depending on the vigor of the illegal poaching industry (which still thrives), but the most recent estimates mean there are more tigers in zoos and circuses around the world than there are in the wild.

The tiger's habitat ranges from the woodlands of Siberia to the tropical evergreen and deciduous forests of southern Asia; from the mangrove swamps of the Sunderbans to the dry thorn forests of northwestern India and the tall grass jungles beneath the Himalayas.

The surviving subspecies are: the Bengal (*Panthea tigris tigris*) of the Indian subcontinent, numbering about 4,500; the Amur or Siberian (*P.t. altaica*) in the Amur river region of Russia and China, and North Korea, (about 450); the Amoy or South China (*P.t. amoyensis*) in south-central China (30–80); the Sumatran (*P.t. sumatrae*) in Sumatra, Indonesia (400–600); and the Indo-Chinese (*P.t. corbetti*) in continental south east Asia (1,000–1,750). The Javan (*P.t. sondaica*) has been extinct since the early 1980s, the Bali (*P. t. balica*) since the 1940s, and the Caspian (*P. t. virgata*) since 1970.

Tiger meat, said to taste of veal, is eaten in Malaya to "cure" debility of the spleen or stomach. Elsewhere in Asia eating tiger parts is supposed to impart the creature's courage and treat a multiplicity of ills. In Taiwan tiger "wine" is made from the bones.

Left: The tiger, like most cats, sharpens its claws by raking them down trees, as this one is doing in the Baudhaugarh National Park, India. Researchers measure scratch heights to estimate tiger sizes but the blazes also mark the animal's territory, as do sprays of urine, feces, and scent deposits.

Right: Facial markings appear symmetrical (particularly above the eyes) but they aren't quite, and individuals are readily identified.

Following pages: This tiger, upset by its own reflection, attacked it with its massive forepaws. The tiger is heavily built with a long muscular body, powerful limbs, and a tail less than half its head-and-body length. Colors vary from reddish-orange to yellow-ochre with creamy white chest, belly, insides of the limbs, throat, muzzle, brows, and whiskers. Stripes vary from gray to black with infinite pattern variations.

Male tigers weigh 400–575 lb (180–260 kg) and females 285–350 lb (130–160 kg) with body lengths of 75–130 inches (190–330 cm) and tails up to 43 inches (110 cm). Average shoulder height is 3½ feet (1.15 m).

Above: Like this Siberian, all tigers love water and will bathe and paddle at every opportunity.

Opposite: This moderately-sized (and drowsy) individual would have been stretched to its limits by tiger hunters of yore. In the days of the Raj it was obligatory for VIP hunters to shoot monsters of 11 feet (3.35 m) or more – though such beasts were exceedingly rare. Accordingly, the more modestly proportioned victim would be tugged vigorously from both ends and measured with a very flexible tape which followed all the contours of the body. Allegedly, a special tape, with only 11 inches to the foot, was kept for Viceroys.

Left: A tiger's roar is a two-part "ooomph-augh," heard most often at mating time but also after a kill and when the beast is patrolling territorial boundaries. Tigers also emit a "pook" sound, made, some observers think, to deceive sambar deer but probably just a mating call.

Above: These sub-adult siblings won't be so friendly once they mature and establish their own territories; then they might fight to the death. Territorial sizes for males (with larger ranges than females) vary according to habitat: from 7½ to 58 sq miles (19–151 sq km) in the prey-rich Royal Chitwan Park, Nepal, up to 385 sq miles (1,000 sq km) in prey-poor Siberia. An individual might travel up to 20 miles (32 km) during a night's hunting.

Previous pages: In Manchuria and Siberia tigers grow thick coats when winter snows lie deep and put on a layer of fat up to 2 inches (5 cm) thick on their bellies and flanks.

Left: The Siberian tiger is the largest of all living terrestrial meat-eaters and no smaller than the saber-toothed tigers of prehistory. The biggest tiger on record is a Siberian male of 1,025 lb (465 kg).

Right: Though persecuted like the rest of its species, the Siberian tiger has largely escaped the attentions of big game hunters like the Maharajah of Surguja who admitted in his dotage in the 1960s that he had shot "only 1,150" Bengal tigers in a lifetime of hunting that began when he was about 10 years old and continued until he was too weak to carry a gun.

165

Previous pages: Tigers eat deer of all sorts but also wild boar, wild pigs, gaur and buffalo, bears, domestic livestock, young elephants, and, occasionally, people. In Siberia they take wolves, lynx, badgers, and dogs. A 550 lb (250 kg) tiger can kill and drag away a 2,200 lb (1,000 kg) gaur and Siberian tigers have been known to eat up to 110 lb (50 kg) at one sitting, although the average in India is 30–40 lb (15–18 kg).

Above: A heavy tiger cannot leap as far as a cougar or leopard so it usually stalks to within 35–65 feet (10–20 m) then rushes, grasping its victim by the back of the neck with its teeth and wrenching it to the ground with its forepaws. If the vertebrae are not crushed it will clamp its jaws around the throat and suffocate its prey.

Opposite: Although its sense of smell is poorer than its sight and hearing, a tiger can identify individual odors. Like other cats, when it wants to get maximum input it will screw up its nose and extend its tongue to expose the scent to a specialized olfactory sensor – Jacobson's organ – in the roof of its mouth.

Left: A Siberian tiger washes down after feeding. Hunters in Siberia believe the tiger can mimic the call of female wapiti during the rutting season, attracting male deer to within killing distance.

171

Opposite: Perhaps licking its lips in anticipation of a meal, this Bengal has to work hard for its food. Not only do prey often fight back – a wild pig has been known to kill a tiger and even water buffalo and gaur occasionally see off their aggressors – but tigers in general are successful only once in every 20 attacks.

Above: A tiger cub suckles from its mother. Most litters comprise 2–3 cubs which open their eyes after a week, begin to eat small quantities of meat at eight weeks and are fully weaned after 5–6 months. A mother moves cubs from the original den at about two months, leading them on foot rather than carrying them in her mouth as many other cats do. Only 50 percent of offspring reach independence (usually at two years) and three-fifths of these fail to establish a territory or to breed. Tigers mate all year and gestation lasts about 102 days.

Right: A healthy individual like this is unlikely to join the ranks of man-eaters, which tend to be older, injured, or sick animals. However, man-eating tigers are fairly common throughout the species' range (but rare in Manchuria and Siberia). In India about 40 people are killed each year, mostly because of loss of habitat and prey and where illegal plantations have been set up in protected areas. By comparison, 1,046 people were killed in India in 1902 when the tiger was more numerous and widespread. Most modern attacks are in the Sunderbans, swamplands along the Bay of Bengal, where woodcutters wear painted masks on the backs of their heads to "face up" to tigers, which usually attack from behind.

BIG CATS OF THE
AMERICAS

CANADIAN LYNXES

— AND —

BOBCATS

The Bobcat (*Lynx rufus*) and the Canadian lynx (*L. canadensis*) are closely related, occupying much the same range and sharing a solitary existence.

The bobcat (sometimes called the red lynx or bay lynx) is slightly smaller and is found from the Canadian border south to Mexico and from coast to coast in a mix of habitats. It is equally happy in semi-desert, swamp, forest, and woodland and even near human habitation.

The Canadian lynx ranges throughout forested areas of Alaska and Canada, and the US states of Montana, Idaho, and Washington. Some are also found in wooded parts of New York, Maine, Oregon, Wyoming, and Colorado. It hunts mostly during the day, as opposed to the bobcat which is active at dawn and dusk.

Where their territories overlap, the more aggressive bobcat forces out its larger cousin, although the lynx is a known predator of the bobcat. However, the lynx rules the roost in areas with heavy snow cover as the thick "galoshes" which come with its winter pelage make it twice as efficient as the bobcat at supporting its weight on snow. Accordingly, the bobcat is not found at elevations over 12,000 feet (3,600 m).

Neither is at any risk of extinction (except the lynx in New Brunswick) and both are still vigorously trapped and shot within a quota system (the bobcat being the most hunted of all the cats).

179

Left: This picture dispels the myth that cats don't like water. The bobcat is so fond of fish that it will lie semi-submerged waiting for a snack to swim by before hooking the unsuspecting creature from the water with a deft swipe of its paw.

Above: Most cats use their tails to aid balance when climbing trees but the bobcat, despite having a stubby tail of just 4–8 inches (11–20 cm), which lends it its name, is surefooted when moving about above ground.

Previous page: It is not just vanity that prompts the bobcat to groom itself so frequently, but more a case of coping with the elements. The beautiful fur coat, which still attracts hunters today, needs to be kept in immaculate condition to remain waterproof.

Left: With a shoulder height of $17\frac{1}{2}$–$23\frac{1}{2}$ inches (45–60 cm) and body length of up to 37 inches (95 cm), the bobcat is smaller than the Canadian lynx; males weigh up to 31 lb (14 kg). Its size varies according to location: those in the north of its range or living in the open are generally larger than those in the south or in forested areas.

Above: Rabbits make up a large part of the bobcat's diet, especially cottontails, which are easier to catch than jackrabbits. Fresh meat is brought back to the den for the kittens and, if they are too young to eat it, they might play with it for a while before the mother eats it herself. The litter usually comprises three or four kittens which are weaned at 10–12 weeks and learn to hunt with their mother shortly after. The kittens, in their turn, are preyed upon by great horned owls.

Right: Like all cats, the bobcat uses facial expressions to communicate emotions – aggression being universally recognized.

Right: Stealth and patience are essential for a successful hunter; add speed and agility and the result is an efficient killing machine. For this snowshoe hare – flushed from its hideout beneath the snow by a bobcat – time is running out if it is to make its escape.

Left: Born blind and helpless, Canadian lynx kittens don't leave their den until they are a month old and it can be up to five months before they are fully weaned. Litter sizes vary and can comprise as many as eight in years when food is abundant.

Above: As the kittens grow up they accompany their mother on hunting trips. Adult lynx hunt alone but during the learning process mother and kittens hunt in line formation. Family life continues in harmony until the following mating season when prospective suitors chase the adolescents away.

Following pages: The characteristic black tip to its short tail distinguishes the lynx from the similar bobcat. The reddish hairs on the rest of its coat are tipped with white, as if touched by frost. This shimmer is how the lynx got its name: from the Greek word *lunx*, meaning "to shine."

Above: With flattened ears adding ferociousness to its snarl, this lynx is clearly issuing a warning to come no closer.

Right: Canadian lynx numbers fluctuate in direct proportion to the available number of snowshoe hares – the lynx's staple diet. This was first noticed through the fluctuating fur returns of the Hudson Bay Company in the 19th century when lynx pelt numbers varied from a record of 36,000 in the best year to a mere 2,000 in the worst.

Adult male lynx grow to a body length of up to 43 inches (110 cm) and a maximum weight of 40 lb (18 kg) and average lifespan for both sexes is about 15 years.

MOUNTAIN LIONS

— AND —

FLORIDA PANTHERS

The mountain lion (*Puma concolor*) – also generally known as the puma or cougar – is very adaptable, ranging from the Canadian Yukon to the southern tip of South America and from seashores to snowy peaks. Any area with sufficient cover and food will provide a suitable habitat: forest, grassland, or swamp. A rocky outcrop or cave provides a safe temporary den but the mountain lion will wander at will throughout its territory, which can be immense: some males have territories extending to 500 square miles (about 1,300 sq km).

Adult males (up to 40 percent bigger than females) grow to a maximum shoulder height of about 30 inches (76 cm), a head-and-body length of 8 feet (2.4 m) and a weight of 225 lb (102 kg). The thick tail – up to 32 inches (82 cm) long in males – is big enough, according to native American folklore, to whip up waves and storms on the Great Lakes but is actually used to aid balance, particularly when making the prodigious jumps for which this cat is renowned. It can cover almost 40 feet (12 m) in a single leap, its unusually long hind legs providing the power.

The Florida panther (*P.c. coryi*), one of 24 sub-species, is the only wild cat living east of the Mississippi. Found in Florida, Arkansas, and Louisiana, it was given protection in 1958, listed as endangered in 1967, and added legal safeguards were introduced in 1978. Like other mountain cats, it lives to about 12 years old in the wild. Males are up to 7 feet (2.1 m) long (including tail) and weigh about 106–148 lb (48–67 kg); females grow to 6 feet (1.8 m) and 66–100 lb (30–45 kg).

Previous pages: A litter of mountain lion cubs can number as many as six but three or four is more common. Weighing 8oz–1lb (226–453g) at birth, the cubs grow rapidly to become energetic bundles of fun.

Opposite: Although they might be weaned at six to seven weeks, cubs remain with their mother for up to two years. The more adventurous might leave home at 15 months, and siblings often stay together for a while before establishing their own solitary lifestyle.

Right: In Argentina, the Gauchos called the mountain lion *amigo del Christiano:* the Christian's friend. According to legend, a young girl called Maldonada got lost while searching for edible roots during an Indian siege of Buenos Aires. She sheltered in a cave and was accepted by the resident mountain lion and her cubs. When she was found and brought back to town at the end of the siege, Maldonada was accused of siding with the Indians and punished by being tied to a tree and left to be eaten by wild animals. The townsmen returned after two nights and a day expecting to bury her remains but instead found her unharmed and guarded by a female mountain lion.

Previous pages: Cubs begin to play after about 10 days or as soon as they open their eyes. The blue eyes of babyhood turn to the typical feline green at four months.

Right: "*Puma concolor*" means puma of one color but the cubs are born with a furry brown coat, ringed tail, and black spots which fade as they grow older. By the time the cubs are half grown the markings will have disappeared.

The grace, beauty, and power of mountain lions led to them being revered by many ancient American civilizations: the Cochiti Indians of New Mexico built shrines in their honor and the ancient city of Cuzco in Peru is said to be laid out in the shape of a puma.

Following pages: Taking advantage of whatever resources they can find in a challenging environment, two juveniles drink from a pool of water caught in the rocks.

Above: The mountain lion is the only plain-colored cat apart from the lion. In the north of its range, the short coat is a grayish-brown but further south it has a reddish tint. The face, throat, and undersides are paler, with black markings around the muzzle. The absence of a mane on skins sold to them by the Indians puzzled early Dutch traders (who assumed the cat to be the same as its African cousin) but the hunters (probably equally puzzled by demands for maned pelts) said the males lived far away in the mountains and were too fierce to be hunted.

Like other cats, the mountain lion sharpens its formidable claws by raking them along wood.

Opposite: "Mountain screamer" is one of dozens of names given to the mountain lion. This chilling howl – like a woman in agony – was sometimes mistaken by early pioneers for the whistle of a river steamer. The eerie, drawn-out cry is actually the mating call of the female in estrus and other vocalizations by both sexes include snarls, yowls, hisses, and purrs – just like huge pet cats. Cubs whistle to attract their mother's attention and she purrs in reply.

Opposite: The dense coat of the mountain lion can keep out snow and wind at altitudes of up to 14,000 feet (4,260 m).

Previous page and above: The mountain lion eats mostly deer (up to 50 a year per adult) but it will happily introduce variety in the form of rabbits, birds, squirrels, and beavers, sometimes adding a sprinkling of frogs, rodents, insects – and even fish. Large prey – killed by a neck-crushing bite – is dragged to a more secure spot before being consumed and, when sated, the lion will bury the remains for future meals. A moose or caribou can last a week or more but the carcass is abandoned if fresh meat is available. Cubs are brought meat from a kill at about six weeks. Their mother then leads them to the carcass to feed and takes them back to the safety of the den when they have eaten. This sets the pattern for the cubs' hunting selection as they will only kill what they have previously been fed by their mother.

Following page: Like the cheetah, the mountain lion can run extremely fast – up to 35 mph (56 kph) over a short distance – but lacks the stamina for a prolonged chase. If a deer manages to evade the lion's first springing attack it stands a good chance of out-running its aggressor.

Opposite: This juvenile Florida panther faces a tough fight for survival. The Florida panther is rarely seen and numbers are believed to have dropped to fewer than 100, making it one of the most endangered mammals of the world.

Above: The Florida panther occupies varied habitats including pinewoods, hardwood forests, and swampy areas but its range is shrinking. Apart from the usual threats of hunting and habitat loss, the Florida panther suffers high losses from road accidents. Tunnels have been built under one of the highways in Florida's panther territory with some success.

Right: A close view of the Florida panther shows the few minor characteristics that differentiate it from the western cougar. The tawny brown coat has some white flecks on the head and shoulders and there is a right-angled crook at the end of the tail, not found on other sub-species. It also has an exaggerated rise of the nasal arch.

216

JAGUARS
— AND OTHER —
SOUTH AMERICAN CATS

Little surprise that powerful cars and fighter aircraft should be named after the spellbinding, spine-tingling jaguar — a brooding presence in what are usually already unnerving environments.

The biggest cat in the Americas, it is found in a mix of habitations including forest, scrub, desert, and savannah (but usually somewhere near water). It ranges from southwest USA to northern Argentina and generally stays in the lowlands below 3,280 feet (1,000 m), but has been seen at almost 12,500 feet (3,800 m). Once found in the north of the United States it has become extinct there and is now absent from Uruguay and the pampas scrubland of Argentina. The Amazon basin rainforest is the key stronghold with population densities as high as one per $5\frac{1}{2}$ sq miles (15 sq km).

The population is thought to be recovering from the depredations of the fur trade (although farmers still persecute the jaguar) and numbers are now put at anything between 15,000 and 23,000.

The jaguar has a large number of smaller wild cats keeping it company in South America — ocelot, margay, jaguarundi, pampas cat, Andean mountain cat, Geoffroy's cat, oncilla, and kodkod — and each has its own peculiar characteristics. Geoffroy's cat (*Oncifelis geoffroyi*), for instance, is one of the great feline swimmers, with one female being seen to cross and re-cross a 100 foot- (30 m) wide, fast-flowing Chilean river at least 20 times in succession. And the closely-related kodkod (*O. guigna*) of Argentina and Chile, with its strangely large feet, is the smallest felid in the Americas, weighing an average of just 5 lb (2.2 kg).

Previous page: The jaguar catches a fish in the same way as a domestic cat – lying in wait then swiping it from the water with its paw. Seeing the eager cat twitching its tail as it lurked at the water's edge, the Indians believed it used it to entice fish to the surface.

Opposite: Jaguars do have a more tiring day than most cats as they are active for up to 14 hours a day rather than being exclusively nocturnal.

Right: Predominantly a forest dweller, the jaguar is an agile climber and will even hunt monkeys by invading their own habitat.

Previous pages: It's easy to confuse a jaguar with a leopard in a zoo, but not in the wild: if the wilderness is in America it must be a jaguar as the leopard is found only in Africa and Asia. The markings are similar but over its back and shoulders the jaguar's spots form rosettes with smaller dots inside.

Above: Turtles are a favorite item on the menu of the water-loving jaguar which has become adept at opening the carapace with its teeth. Another delicacy, if they are available, is turtle eggs, but the jaguar is not that fussy: snake's eggs will do, or even the snake itself.

Opposite: Known throughout Spanish-speaking America as "El tigre," the stocky jaguar is a powerful creature, lacking the grace of the leopard.

Left: Of all the big cats, the jaguar has the most powerful bite in relation to its size. Sometimes going for its victim's throat for a quick kill like other cats, it also uses these strong teeth to pierce the skull, which its cousins seldom do.

The jaguar's size, head-and-body length of 44–95 inches (112–241 cm), and weight of 80–384 lb (36–158 kg) vary enormously according to its range. The largest are found in Chaco, Argentina, and the Mato Grosso while the smallest are in Central America.

Above: The males usually spend only 4–5 days with the female during the mating season although they have been known to linger around to meet their offspring and help to provide the cubs with food.

Opposite: Many folk legends are told about the jaguar and, like all tales about enigmatic creatures (less is known about this elusive cat than its Eastern cousins), they are elaborated with each telling. At one extreme jaguars were said to come out of the forest to play with Indian children; at the other the Mayan people believed it to be a savage and powerful god that guarded the way for the sun as it traveled beneath the earth each night. They built a vast temple to their jaguar god in the Guatemalan city of Tikal and their high priests wore jaguar robes. The Peruvian highland Indians also revered the creature, and carved jaguar faces into the walls of their temples.

Opposite: Occasionally jaguars have been known to take human prey but, fortunately, never seem to acquire the taste sufficiently to become man-eaters in the same way as some other great cats.

Above: In the denser rainforests melanistic jaguars are more likely to occur than in more open terrain. Sometimes black, sometimes a dark chestnut brown, these black panthers, as they are also known, still have their spots – but these can only be seen when the sun shines directly on their fur.

Above: For the first few days after giving birth the mother jaguar will stay with her sightless cubs, guarding them fiercely. They will venture from their den after about six weeks and stay with their mother for two years. Sensibly, the female usually waits until the young have left home before beginning another litter.

Opposite: As with other big cats in Asia and Africa, the presence of man has had a profound impact on the population and distribution of the jaguar. Although it is still hunted, despite being on the list of endangered species since the 1970s, it is principally the destruction of the jaguar's habitat that has caused the most significant decline in population in recent years.

Opposite: Mainly a nocturnal creature, the exquisite ocelot (*Leopardus pardalis*) spends the day resting or sleeping in the safety of a comfortable tree. This slender cat has a long body – up to 53 inches (136 cm) – and its ringed or barred tail adds another 11–17½ inches (28–45 cm).

Above: Like many cats the ocelot will catch fish by scooping them from the water with its paw, but fish are a rare treat as the typical diet is made up of small mammals, birds, and reptiles.

Following pages: The ocelot is generally acknowledged to be one of the most beautiful of the smaller cats. Its striking markings are displayed on a background of varying color from creamy white through tawny yellow to a reddish hue, and no two animals are identical. Now a protected species, the ocelot was hunted almost to extinction to feed the fashion for fur coats. Thirteen of these stunning creatures were sacrificed to enable one woman to parade in their skins.

As well as facing death for the sake of the fur trade or to protect the farmer's chickens, the female ocelot was often killed so her kittens could be captured and sold as pets.

Opposite: One of the ocelot's hunting techniques is to move slowly through its cover, stopping when catching sight of its prey before stalking its victim until the opportunity for a final pounce.

Right: All cats use facial expressions and postures to communicate moods and this ocelot shows confusion or suspicion by holding its ears out to the side.

Left: Probably only monkeys or squirrels are more at home in the trees than the margay (*Leopardus wiedi*). This forest dweller spends more time in the trees than on the ground, its flexible ankle joints allowing it to climb down a trunk head first, and hang from branches. Hunting usually takes place among the branches and monkeys, lizards, birds, and other arboreal creatures are eaten where they are caught. However, if the prey leaves the trees, the acrobatic margay will leap like a leopard directly onto its victim without touching the ground.

Opposite: The striking margay can be mistaken for the ocelot or the oncilla (*L. tigrinus*), sometimes called the little spotted cat. The markings are similar in all three but the margay falls between the two in size hence its other common name of "little" or "tree" ocelot. Unfortunately, it is nevertheless considered to be large enough to hunt for its fur, even though 15 pelts are needed to make one coat.

Above: A margay cub is usually an only child, with litters seldom numbering more than one. Weighing about 1lb (450g) at birth, it is about four times the size of a domestic kitten.

Previous pages: An essential aid to balance, the margay's tail represents about 70 percent of its total length and can be as long as 20 inches (51 cm) on larger individuals. This slender cat, weighing 6½–20 lb (3–9 kg) and with a body-and-tail length of 18–31 inches (46–79 cm), can grasp branches with both hind- and fore-paws and has been seen to hang monkey-like from one paw.

Right: Cat's eyes have long given rise to superstitions, and the large eyes of the margay are more eerie than most. (The Chinese once thought, not without some justification, that the pupil size changed according to the position of the sun, and would look into a cat's eyes to tell the time.)

Left: Quite different in appearance from other small cats, the jaguarundi (*Herpailurus yagouarundi*) has pupils which are not slits but rounded, like pantherine cats. Its sleek coat comes in two color phases — one chestnut brown and the other grayish black — and litters can contain kittens of both hues. Weighing 6½–20 lb (3–9 kg), and with a head-and-body length of 20–30 inches (51–77 cm), the jaguarundi is a similar size to the margay.

Above: It's not difficult to see why the Germans call the jaguarundi "weasel cat," its musteline looks leading Mexicans to call it "otter cat." Like most cats, this species can climb trees, but its slender body allows it to move easily through the undergrowth and it hunts mainly on the ground.

Opposite: The jaguarundi makes a tame, affectionate pet but its natural instincts mean it is a danger to domestic poultry, even when on a lead. These instincts were put to good use by native South Americans, who kept jaguarundis to control rodents around their homes.

Above: Although mainly inhabiting grasslands as its name suggests, the pampas cat (*Lynchailurus colocolo*) is at home in open woodland and high mountain areas up to 16,400 feet (5,000 m). Its coloring varies according to location and in the high Andes the coat is a silver-gray with ruddy brown stripes and spots, similar to the rare Andean mountain cat (*Oreailurus jacobita*). At lower levels the coat is often a yellowish-brown, tan, or even black. Whatever the color, the pampas cat has a 2¾-inch (7 cm) dorsal mane which it can fluff up in anger.

Opposite: The pampas cat is not much larger than a domestic cat but, at 6½–8 lb (3–3.7 kg) it is rather heavier and stockier. The bushy, black-ringed tail is 12 inches (30 cm) long, approximately a third of its total length.

BIBLIOGRAPHY & REFERENCES

Brett, Caroline: Wild Cats (Boxtree, London) 1992

Guggisberg, C.A.W.: Wildcats of the World (David & Charles, Newton Abbot) 1975

Mountfort, Guy: Saving the Tiger (Michael Joseph, London) 1981

Ricciuti, Edward R.: The Wild Cats (The Ridge Press) 1979

Seidensticker, John: Tigers (Colin Baxter, Grantown-on-Spey) 1996

Tomkies, Mike: Wildcats (Whittet Books) 1991

Animal Diversity Web: www.animaldiversity.ummz.umich.edu

BBC News: www.bbc.co.uk/1/hi

Big Cats Online: http://dspace.dial.pipex.com/town/plaza/abf90/bco

CanTeach: www.canteach.ca/elementary/africa

Cat Survival Trust, The: http://members.aol.com/_ht_a/cattrust/index.htm

IUCN Cat Specialist Group: http://lynx.uio.no/lynx/catsgportal/20_catsg-website/home/index_en.htm

Lady Wildlife: www.ladywildlife.com

Lioncrusher: www.lioncrusher.com

Snow Leopard Conservancy: www.snowleopardconservancy.org/index.htm

Wildlife Protection Society of India: www.wpsi-india.org

World Wildlife Fund, Nepal Program: www.wwfnepal.org

*All web references as at 11/14/2005

CREDITS

The publisher would like to thank Photolibrary.com for kindly providing the photographs for this book. We would also like to thank the following for kind permission to reproduce their photographs.

LIONS

Bailey, Adrian 8-9,28-29,32-33. Cox, Daniel 38. Dani 46. Fischer, Berndt 30,34-35. Hamblin, Mark 24. Hill, Mike 12-13,42-43. Hoffman, Barbara, Von/AA 44. Newman, Owen 21. Osolinski, Stan 16, 31. Packwood, Richard ,25,26-27,36-37. Powles, Mike 18-19. Rosing, Norbert 10-11,39. Deeble M and Stone V 22-23. Shay, Alistair 14-15. Staebler, Gabriela/OPAKIA 20. Tipling, David 45. Turner, Steve 40-41. Zandbergen, Adriadne Van 17.

CHEETAHS

Bailey, Adrian 56,60-61. Bartlett, Des & Jen/SAL 80-81. Breed, David 6,54-55,72. Cox, Daniel 66-67. Hill, Mike 62. Gallo Images 64, 65. Jackson, Tim 70-71. Nunnington, Bob 52. Osolinski, Stan 48-49, 58,79. Packwood, Richard 48. Plage, Mary 59. Rosing, Norbert 50-51,63,68,74-75,76,77,82

LEOPARDS

Bannister, Anthony 100. Carey, Alan & Sandy 111,112,116. Cox, Daniel 118. Deeble, M & Stone, V 102-103. Gallo Images 94. Hill, Mike 92,117. Ifa-Bilderteam 84-85. Norbert, Rosing 88-89,96. Powles, Mike 101. Turner, Steve 87,91,95,98-99. Stone, Lynn/AA 114-115. Weimann, Peter/AA 110. Winslow, Robert 105,107,108-109. Wothe, Konrad/AA 90

WILD CATS, LYNXES & SMALLER CATS

Austermann, Miriam 133. Cox, Daniel 124-125. Dick, Michael 135,143. Dragesco-Joffre, Alain 120-121, 128,132. Hamblin, Mark 149. Henry, Philippe 144. Jones. Adam 130. Kenney, Brian 122. Leszczynski, Zig/AA 139. McDonald, Joe 123. Osolinski, Stan 127. Reinhard, Hans/OKAPIA 147. Rosin, Norbert 148. Senanai, Krupakar 104-141. Sewell, Michael 136-137. Stouffier Enterprises/AA 134. Turner, Steve 131. Wothe, Konrad 146,150. Wright, Belinda 138

TIGERS

A & M Shar/AA 159. Bennett, Bob 6,165,169. Carey, Alan & Sandy 156-157,158,168,170. Cox, Daniel 164. Hill, Mike 152,172. Jorge Sierra, Antinolo 155. Leszczynski, Zig/AA 156-157,160. Neep, Elliot 173. Powles, Mike 174-175. Satyendra, Tiwari 154,161,166-167. Su Keren 162-163.

BIG CATS OF NORTH AMERICA

Bennett, Bob 181,214. Carey, Alan & Sandy 196-197,235. Chelman, John 233. Cole, Ken 218. Colombini, Fabio 230. Cooney, Judd 185. Cox, Daniel 2,178-179,180,184,188,190,193,194,198,199,200-201,203,204-205,206,210,212-213,215. Fogden, Michael 243. Foster, Carol Farneti 221,226. Gordon, Nick 224,232. Kemp, Richard & Julia 253. Kenney, Brian 182,216-217,238,242. Lauber, Lon E 192. Marty Stouffer Prods/AA 187. Michael, Dick 248,252. OSF 222. Partridge Films Ltd 240-41,244-5,250,251. Pointier, John 234. Rosing, Norbert 231. Rue, Leonard Lee 211. Scheidermeyer, Frank 239. Stone, Lynn 225. Turner, Steve 189,207. Ulrich, Tom 208-209. Von Hoffmann, Barbara 229. Weimann, Peter 228,236-237. Wu, Norbert 220

Front of jacket image Mike Powles; Back flap image: Kjell Sandved